My First Book
about
JESUS

by Walter Wangerin, Jr.
illustrated by Jim Cummins

Rand McNally & Company
Chicago • New York • San Francisco

Library of Congress Cataloging in Publication Data

Wangerin, Walter.
  My first book about Jesus.

  Summary: Recounts events in the life of Jesus from his
birth to his appearance three days after his death.
  1. Jesus Christ—Biography—Juvenile literature.
2. Christian biography—Palestine—Juvenile literature.
[1. Jesus Christ.   2. Bible stories—N.T.]   I. Cummins, Jim,
1914–   ill.   II. Title.
BT302.W235   1983   232.9′01   82-10218
ISBN 0-528-82403-1

First printing, 1983

To the Adults Who Love the Children:

Most of the sweet, victorious tales in this world are fairy tales. In them the child is allowed to imagine evil overcome.

But there is one tale which is no one's imagination, which is true and therefore very powerful: the story of Jesus. Here we do not say to the child, "Imagine." We say, "Believe!" We do not pretend that a little girl had a fairy godmother to help her. Rather, we announce in fact that a real child has a real God to help and to love her.

You, my child, there is a victory for you!

The story of Jesus. It is a beautiful tale, a terrible tale, and then again a tale more beautiful than any other. For, that God should come to love is beautiful. That he should fight the devil, suffer the hatred of a sinful world, and die—these things are too true (as children know) and terrible. But wait! That he should rise to life again, triumphant over evil, and that he should wish to share the triumph with his children is the most beautiful news of all.

There is a victory for all of us.

Walter Wangerin, Jr.
Easter Week, 1983

The baby Jesus was born this way:

An angel came to a woman and said, "God loves you, Mary."

Bright and sudden as the sun was this angel, so Mary was frightened.

"No, don't be afraid, dear Mary," said the angel, "for this is what the love of God will do. You will have a baby, a child, a boy as great as any king."

Mary said, "But I have no husband yet."

The angel said, "With God nothing is impossible. When this babe is born, name him Jesus. He shall be the Son of God."

Mary wondered at the angel's words and smiled to think that she would be a mother.

"Then let it be," she said. "Ah, let it be."

A man named Joseph married her. In time they traveled
from Nazareth to Bethlehem, a long journey and difficult
afoot, for they went among the hills. When they came to
the tiny town of Bethlehem, Mary was groaning; the baby
was coming.

Joseph knocked on doors, looking for a room, asking for a bed, for the baby was coming. But no one had a room for them. So he took his Mary to a stable, and there she bore her baby, and the baby cried, but she wrapped him in swaddling clothes and laid him in a manger.

Tired Mary, pretty Mary: She touched the baby's cheek, and she said, "Jesus."

That night shepherds were watching sheep in the fields, under dim and distant stars. Then, as bright and sudden as the sun, an angel appeared, and the shepherds were afraid.

"No need to fear good news!" said the angel. "Listen: Christ the Lord was born in Bethlehem. Go, look for him. Look for a baby in swaddling clothes, and lying in a manger."

Suddenly the night was ablaze with a thousand angels, flying and crying aloud, "Glory, glory to God, and peace to his people on earth!"

When they departed, the stars alone were left, dim and
distant in the darkness; but the night was sweet with promise.

"Let's go," said the shepherds, "and worship this child."
Right quickly they ran to Bethlehem; but when they found
the stable, right slowly they went in. "Oh" and "ah" they
said for wonder, their eyes shining with tears, for they were
looking at the Savior.

The baby Jesus grew.

Wise men, strangers who could read the meaning of the stars, came riding from the East. By a star they found the house where Jesus lived. And then, as though he were a king, they gave him gifts, gold, frankincense, and myrrh.

And the baby grew.

When Jesus was twelve years old, his parents took him
to the holy city of Jerusalem. For a week they worshiped
God there, praying, laughing, eating the feast of the Passover,
and enjoying their friends and relatives. Then Mary and
Joseph traveled home again, a long trip, a large crowd all
around them.

When evening came, they called for Jesus, but he didn't
answer. He was nowhere in the crowd. Afraid for him, they
hurried back to Jerusalem.

"Jesus? Jesus, where are you? Our little boy is lost."

After three days they found the boy sitting in the temple among the teachers. Not only was he asking questions, he was answering them, too, so that the old men wondered at his wisdom.

"Jesus!" Mary scolded. "We were worried about you!"

"Why, Mother?" he said. "Didn't you know that I would be in my Father's house?"

Sometimes Mary stroked the boy's unwrinkled forehead. "Ah, Jesus. What will happen to you, Jesus?" She worried because an old man once had told her that Jesus would do things great and dangerous—and she loved the child.

Time passed. The years went by. And in the end that old man's words proved true. Jesus did the greatest, most dangerous thing of all: He saved his people from their sins. Here is that story.

A man named John announced that Jesus was coming.
"Get ready for the coming of the Lord," he cried in the wilderness. John wore camel's hair. He ate locusts and wild honey. And when the people came to him, he took them into the river where he washed them. This was a special washing called baptism, for it showed that the people were sorry for their sins. Thus they prepared for the Lord.

"O people," said John, "the one who is coming is so much greater than I that I should not even tie his shoes."

One day Jesus stood by John and said, "Baptize me."

But John recognized him. "No," he said. "Rather you should baptize me."

"I must do everything perfectly," said Jesus. "Come, John. Do it."

So, the man who had no sin was baptized—and suddenly the sky split open. The Holy Spirit came down like a dove and perched on Jesus' shoulder, and a voice thundered in the heavens, saying, "This is my beloved Son, with whom I am well pleased."

Immediately the Spirit gave Jesus a frightful command. "Go," it said. "Go alone into the wilderness, where you will meet the Devil."

For forty days Jesus walked the stony wilderness, eating
nothing. Then the Devil came.

"Ho, ho!" said the Devil. "Is the Son of God hungry?
Well, turn these stones to bread and eat."

"No, that would be a sin," said Jesus, "for no one lives
by bread alone. We live by the words of God."

The Devil frowned. He snatched Jesus away to the
highest tower of the temple. "If you are the Son of God," he
hissed, "prove it. Jump! See if God will catch you."

But Jesus said, "It is a sin to test the Lord God."

The Devil frowned harder. By a furious wind he blew poor Jesus to the top of a mountain, where they could see all the lands and nations and kingdoms of this world. "Bow down and worship me," he whispered, "and I'll give you all you see."

But Jesus said, "The worst sin of all is to worship anyone but God. Devil, Devil, get away from me!" cried Jesus.

So Jesus was tempted terribly, but he did not sin.

After that Jesus returned to the river, and John pointed at him, saying, "Look! This is the Lamb of God who takes away the sin of the world. Are you ready, all you people? Here is the Lord whom I told you about."

Jesus said, "For the work that I do, I will have no house, no bedroom, and no bed. Foxes sleep in holes. In nests the birds do sleep. But I won't even have a pillow for my head."

Jesus said, "For my work, I won't need money, no possessions for me. And I shall have enemies, people who won't understand how much I love.

"But," said Jesus, "I shall have friends as well, and I will teach them. I will teach them to love one another even as I love them."

So one day, as he walked along the sea, he called to the fishermen working there. There was one man stronger than the others, Peter; and beside him was his brother Andrew. To these two, Jesus said, "Follow me."

There was one man gentler than the others, John; and beside him, his brother James. To these, too, Jesus said, "Follow me." And all four left their boats, their nets, their families, their jobs; and they followed Jesus everywhere.

Jesus didn't take wise people or rich people. He asked a tax collector to follow him. Plain people. Simple working people. Altogether, twelve men came to follow him.

"You are my disciples," he said. "You will be my friends."

So Jesus began his glorious work. And what a mighty worker he was, yet how tender his hands on those who were hurting.

There came a man whose skin was white as paper and peeling from his bones. He had the disease called leprosy.

"If you want to," he said to Jesus, "you can heal me."

"I want to," said Jesus. He put his hands on the sick man's face. "Be healed." And soon his skin was ruddy, smooth, and well again.

All the people said, "Did you see what Jesus can do? He is most certainly a mighty man!"

Crowds of people began to gather around Jesus, bringing
sick children, blind men, crippled women, all the troubles of a
troubled, troubled world.

And Jesus healed them, every one, because he
loved them.

Jesus was teaching in a house so full of people that no one else could get in. But here came four men carrying a fifth man, one who could not walk because his legs were stiff as sticks. "How will we come to Jesus," they said, "so that he might heal our friend?" But these were clever men. They climbed to the roof, where they made a hole right over Jesus. Then they let their friend down, by ropes, into the room.

"Well, hello," said Jesus when he saw the paralyzed man in front of him. And then he said, "My son, your sins are forgiven."

But people were angered to hear that. "Who do you think you are—God?" they said. "Only God can forgive sins."

Jesus said, "This is the very reason why I came. I came to forgive sins. But to prove that I have the power to forgive, I will heal his sickness, too." To the man he said, "Get up and walk." And immediately that man jumped up and kicked his healthy heels and walked.

The people said, "There is no one mightier than Jesus."

But some of the people glared at him. Jesus was right. He had enemies, now, as well as friends.

Jesus said to his disciples, "I know what you think. You think that you should love your friends and hate your enemies. But I say to you that you should love your enemies as well; and for the person who hurts you, you should pray!

"Listen to a story about a man from a group of people everyone hated. Those people were not well to do. Their ways were different. And so they were hated. That man was a Samaritan.

"Once a traveler was walking from Jerusalem to Jericho by a winding and treacherous road. All at once robbers leaped out of the hills, attacked the traveler, stole his clothes and his money, and left him dying.

"Soon a priest came along that road. He heard the traveler groaning, but he gathered his robes and rushed away, not helping at all.

"Then a Levite passed, a very religious man; but he pretended that he saw nothing and slipped by on the other side.

"Finally," said Jesus, "the Samaritan came riding, the man whom everyone hated. He knew about hurting. When he saw the wounded traveler, he knelt in the dust, poured medicines upon the cuts, bandaged the bruises, and brought the poor man to an inn. 'Whatever it costs,' he told the innkeeper, 'I will pay until the man is healed.'

"This good Samaritan," said Jesus, "knew well how to love."

And Jesus said, "The greatest commandment is that you love God. The second greatest commandment is that you do to other people what you hope they do to you." Even so did Jesus teach his dear disciples.

The crowds followed Jesus wherever he went, for God was with him. The life in Jesus was like light to the people. And, oh, how they needed his life!

"Jesus! Jesus! Please, dear Jesus!" cried a man in trouble.

The crowds let him through, whispering, "Poor Jairus, he has such a great need."

The man named Jairus grabbed Jesus at his knees and wept. "My little girl is sick," he said. "Just twelve years old, the child I love! Dying, dying, the daughter I cry for! Please, please come and heal her!"

Jesus lifted Jairus to his feet, and together they tried to hurry home. But hundreds of people made the hurrying difficult and very slow. When they came to the house, then, bad news was waiting for them.

"Too late," said the doctor. "Don't bother Jesus anymore. The little girl is dead."

Like rain the tears ran down the face of this father. But Jesus said, "Jairus, do not be afraid. Believe!" He led Jairus into his house, but here was another problem: All of the relatives were weeping and wailing and blowing their noses. Such noises they made of their sorrow!

Jesus said, "Why are you crying? The girl is sleeping, not dead."

"Ho, ho!" the people laughed at him. "We know death when we see it."

"Out," spoke Jesus to the useless relatives. "Get out!" They obeyed his command; then Jesus smiled at Jairus. "Show me your daughter," he said.

Pale as snow the little girl lay, and very, very still.

Jesus took the child's icy hand and whispered, "Little girl, get up." And that is what she did. She coughed. The color burned her cheek. She opened her eyes, and she sat up.

Bright, joyful, were the tears on a father's face, now; and Jesus said, "Find her some food and feed her."

Jesus asked his disciples, "Do you know who I am?"

"The Christ!" cried Peter. "You are the Son of God."

"Yes," said Jesus. "Now, do you also know why I came into the world?"

"Why, to be a king," said Peter. "And we will fight beside you, winning war after war." Peter was strong as stone.

"I am a King," said Jesus, "but not in this world. In this world I am a servant. Please listen to the most important lesson of all: I came to die. In Jerusalem my enemies shall hurt me; but neither you nor I shall fight back. Then they will kill me. After three days I will rise from the dead."

Strong Peter hurt to hear these words. "Never!" he shouted. "This should never happen to you!"

But Jesus said, "O Peter, only the Devil would stop me! I must give my life away that others might live forever."

Now Jesus began to travel the road to Jerusalem, and always the crowds surrounded him.

Here came fathers with children and mothers with wishes: "Maybe Jesus will touch my daughter, will kiss my son, and maybe he will bless them."

"No! No chance of that," said strong Peter, waving these parents away. "Can't you see how busy Jesus is?"

But Jesus covered Peter's mouth to make him quiet. "Peter, Peter," he said. "The greatest people in the kingdom of heaven are *children*. Let them come to me. Don't ever keep them away!"

Then Jesus hugged the children, kissed them sweetly, loved them deeply, and blessed them. They were his.

Crowds. The crowds that followed Jesus grew to multitudes. Thousands sat to hear his stories. Thousands lined the streets when he passed through Jericho. And when he called to the dead man Lazarus and when that man walked out of his grave alive, thousands and thousands cheered so that they made the valleys ring.

And that is why the enemies of Jesus feared him—
because of these crowds.

"Jesus might turn his thousands into armies," they said.
"He might attack the Roman soldiers—or fight us! Oh, what
riots he could start, and then our nation would be in serious
trouble, and we would lose our power.

"So," they said, "we'll get Jesus before he gets us. Better
for one to die than many."

Then came the day when Jesus rode into Jerusalem. On a donkey he came, both lordly and lowly at once, and the multitudes thundered their praises of him.

"Blessed is he who comes in the name of the Lord!" they roared. Coats went down like carpets, branches went up like flags, and the children chanted, "Hosanna to the Son of David!"

His enemies screamed, "Tell them to shut their mouths!"

But Jesus said, "If these were still, the stones themselves would sing, and the rocks roar out my name."

Through the city he went, straight to the temple, where he saw men buying and selling for profit. "No!" cried Jesus. He was furious. "Oh, no!" he scolded while he tipped the tables, set animals free, and whipped the people from the temple. "God's house is a house of prayer," he cried, "but you have made it a den of robbers!"

His enemies watched, grinding their teeth in rage.
"That's it," they growled. "That is the last thing Jesus shall
do. Now we must get rid of him."

All that week they awaited their chance to arrest him.
They wanted to find him alone, apart from the crowds.
Finally, on Thursday, the dreadful thing happened. And this
is the way that the Lord Jesus died.

In sadness Jesus ate a final supper with his disciples. "Remember," he said. "Remember to love one another as I love you." Then he and Peter and John and James and the others walked through the night until they came to a little garden called Gethsemane. Jesus went in alone; alone he groaned for sorrow; alone he prayed to God. "I wish these things would not have to happen," he prayed. "But if you want them to, my God, then let them be. Ah, let them be."

It was in the garden that Jesus' enemies found him. They tied his hands, and all the disciples ran away, away, away.

"What shall we do with him?" demanded the high priest.

And Jesus' enemies said, "He is guilty, so he should die. Let him die!"

Jesus bowed his head, saying nothing.

They dragged him to the governor, where they screamed in an ugly rage, "Crucify this dangerous man! Crucify him!"

Jesus said nothing. The governor said, "Do as you please."

And so the enemies had their way. The prisoner was given into the hands of the Roman soldiers. On a hill outside Jerusalem, this sinful world hung its Lord Jesus upon a cross. "Father, forgive them," he sighed, "they know not what they do."

At noon the sky went blacker than night. Then, three hours later, Jesus raised his voice. "It is finished!" he cried. He dropped his head upon his breast. He breathed out. And he died.

How sad were his disciples. Strong Peter was sad, and
sad were the women who had traveled with him.

All Saturday, while Jesus lay inside his grave, his friends
would look on one another and weep because it seemed
as if the enemies had won.

But everything, *everything*, happened just as Jesus said it
would; and the last thing of all was the best—for this was
the glory of God.

Early Sunday morning, when the women walked to his grave to perfume the body of Jesus, behold! They found the grave wide open—and empty. No body at all was there!

But here was an angel, as bright and sudden as the sun, smiling on them. "You came to find Jesus," he said, "but he is not here. Look! He has risen from the dead, exactly as he said he would!"

The women started to cry; but this time they cried for happiness.

That same evening the Lord Jesus himself, in the flesh
and truly alive, came into the room where his disciples
were gathered.

"Peace be with you," he said to them.

At first they were terrified, for it might have been a
ghost. But Jesus showed them the scars in his hands, and
they knew that this was their Lord indeed. "Peace to you,"
he said again.

How they laughed and clapped their hands. How loudly
they shouted their gladness.

And Jesus said, "Now you must go into all the world and
preach the Good News of the forgiveness of sins. Then
people will believe that I am the Christ, and believing, they
shall have life in my name."

"And lo," said Jesus to his friends, "I am with you always—even to the end of time."

About the Author

Walter Wangerin, Jr., is the minister of a small inner-city church in Evansville, Indiana. He is also an author of national renown. His works include articles, reviews, poetry, plays, and several books for children. His first novel, *The Book of the Dun Cow,* was named Best of Young Adult Books-1978 by the *New York Times;* won the American Library Association's Notable Book Award; and in paperback, received the American Book Award, 1980.

Mr. Wangerin was born in Portland, Oregon. In addition to a Master of Divinity degree from Christ Seminary Seminex, he earned a master's degree in English and did advanced studies in medieval English literature at Miami University of Ohio. He has also produced and announced a radio show in St. Louis, taught at several universities, worked with an inner city boys club, and traveled with migrant farm workers.

Mr. Wangerin now lives in Evansville with his wife and four children. In addition to his pastoral duties, he devotes part of each day to his writing.

My First Book About Jesus marks the author's second book for Rand McNally. Previously he wrote *The Bible: Its Story for Children.*